A Pho‹

Our Lady of ....

Claire Riche

S⚙CCIONES

ISBN: 9781982942748

Design & formatting by Socciones Editoria Digitale
www.socciones.co.uk

Personal Thanks

Jesus and Mary, whose direction I felt throughout.

Peter Lloyd, for his proof reading and fantastic constructive criticism.

Ray Gallet, for photo collection and acting as computer help desk.

Philip Knight, Keith Bearne and countless friends who believed in me.

Photograph acknowledgements

Fr. Vitalis MSP Our Lady of Jasna Gora.

Peter Murnaghan Our Lady's Fleur de Lys in Liskeard Town Shield.

Other photos courtesy of Philip Knight and Ray Gallet.

Return to Ladye Park by David Whittley. Oil on canvas, 2001.

This was painted as a commission to be based on the portrayal of
the Virgin Mary on a Liskeard civic Mural in AD 2000.

David Whittley's own interpretation of the painting:

The border represents the Celtic origins of the shrine. The design
itself is a symbol of life, with its complicated journey between
earthly life and spirituality. This is also reflected by the colours, the
green of earth and the gold of the spirit, which edge the path to the
chapel.

(Mary is the fountain of salvation (Psalm 36:9)

Life Journey - Vyaj an Bwynans. Coloured sketch by David Whittley. Referred to in detail in Chapter Six- Evangelisation.

Contents

Introduction

More than 15 years ago, I agonised over whether I should record the information which I had gathered over the previous 40 years, concerning attempts to revive a pre-reformation shrine to the Blessed Virgin Mary in Liskeard, Cornwall.

As I was the one person who had been party to the many pilgrimages, incidents, and information gathering that had taken place during that time, I was well placed to chronicle this for future generations.

I had never previously written anything, so it was not my intention to be published. I simply wanted to record it in one place so that future generations would be able to access it. That dossier of information ended up, six months later, as a book, *The Lost Shrine of Liskeard,* published by Saint Austin Press[1]. It was distributed throughout the world and, to my great surprise, very soon sold out.

I felt my duty was done. I had, by then, moved away from Cornwall. If God did have a plan to revive the shrine further, it would probably not be in my lifetime. As the Bible tells us, God's time is not our time: "With the Lord a day is like a thousand years, and a thousand years are like a day." (2 Peter 3:8-9). I knew Jesus and Mary would call people to continue interest in the shrine until someone else was called to its full restoration. I would no longer be needed and, doubtless, be called elsewhere.

Our Lady, however, seemed to have other plans. It was as though she wanted her story with reference to Liskeard to be held in one place. Future generations would then be able to consult *The Lost Shrine of Liskeard*, as well as another chronicle of events.

In the years following the publication of *The Lost Shrine of Liskeard,* many other intriguing events began to take place and, despite living out of the county, I was drawn into them.

Over the years, several people asked me when I planned to write the next book. I always laughed and said: "Never! The first was written in spite of me. The next, if there is one, will be compiled by someone else."

People persisted. "But you are the link!", they would say, to which I always replied: "No! Our Lady is the link. She will work it out if she wants to."

On 15 August 2016, when the same question was posed to me, I started thinking again. Who knows? If I record my experiences again, they may be of use to someone else in the future.

An hour later, I found myself in the Co-op in Liskeard buying a large blue notebook, on which I inscribed these words: "Our Lady of Liskeard." The next morning, I woke up and started writing. I continued to do this for 30 minutes every morning. This account is the result.

Chapter One
Liskeard

Liskeard is a market town in South East Cornwall, 18 miles from Plymouth, on the southern edge of Bodmin Moor, with a history stretching back to time immemorial.

Prior to the coming of Christianity, legend has it that Liskeard was the seat of Kerrid, a great pagan goddess of love and eternal youth. This was not the bodily eternal youth, as sought after today, but the eternal youth of immortality.

She took her powers via a cauldron, which was said to be her well, from a higher being. She was linked to the Cretan god Ker, a god of death in life, who appeared in the form of a bee that brings the sting of death, but leads to new life.

Her seat, or shrine, became so important that the town which grew up around was called *Lys Kerrid*: Cornish for *Court of Kerrid*. This is the Liskeard we now know.

It is thought Christianity came to Cornwall much earlier than to other parts of England, and certainly earlier than St Augustine in 597AD. It may have arrived as early as 1AD via tin traders travelling to and from the Middle East. Sailors are renowned story tellers. It would seem inconceivable that tales were not told of the charismatic preacher, whose followers were claiming was alive after being crucified to death. There are even documented legends of Jesus himself travelling to Cornwall with his uncle, Joseph of Arimathea. The first Christians in Cornwall doubtless refrained from trying to evangelise the Kerrid worshippers. She was too much part of their culture. However, the situation began to change when Christian missionaries from Ireland arrived.

The old pagan wells were renamed after Christian saints. However, since Kerrid's well was so well known and loved, it was believed, according to tradition, that no saint but the Virgin Mary could persuade locals to give up their beloved Kerrid. Therefore, it became Our Lady's well.

A decision was then taken to build a chapel near to Kerrid's well so that locals, accustomed to visiting her *Lys*, could instead visit Jesus in the Blessed Sacrament and revere Mary his mother there. Many years later, the discovery of the remains of a first millennium chapel appeared to show the chapel was actually built surrounding the well.

The plan to divert locals away from Kerrid to Our Lady clearly worked. Perhaps Our Lady simply made herself known to them in order to lead worshippers to her Son. Our Lady of the Park became so renowned that the spot was adopted by royalty and became a chantry chapel within the hunting lodge of the Duke of Cornwall.

At the Reformation, all Catholic practices were banned throughout the land, even in royal households. Statues and religious art were destroyed and churches ransacked.

The shrine and surrounding land were converted to pasture. Attempts were made to eradicate any memory of this once popular pilgrimage spot. Even history books were rewritten. A covenant was put on the land which forbade religious services of any kind to be held there for 400 years.

However, one small clue to its former secret did remain. The farm which was established was called "Ladye Park" and this ensured that memory of its past importance was kept alive amongst local families. Our Lady's renown was not extinguished. In each generation, whilst some passed this heritage on to their children, it was rarely spoken about openly.

In 1955, Dr. Margaret Pollard, an intelligent, gifted Cornish bard and historian, was living in Truro. She had converted to Catholicism a few years earlier and held a particular love for the Blessed Mother. Since her conversion, she had dedicated herself to introduce as many of her friends as possible, particularly children, to shrines of Our Lady around the world. She organised pilgrimages and holidays to popular shrines such as Fatima, Lourdes and Aylesford. However, she had never visited Liskeard and only knew the town as a train

2

station on the way to London.

On 2 November 1955, something happened to Dr. Pollard which she would remember for the rest of her life.

Although she was a wealthy woman, Dr. Pollard lived a frugal life and lived in a very modest flat with her husband, in Truro. On this day, at 5pm, she suddenly noticed a lady sitting in her antiquated arm chair. Dr. Pollard explains what happened next:

"She was dressed in a variety of shades of blue, full flowing draperies and she wore a tiara-shaped crown with projecting rays that appeared to be jewelled with dull opaque stones like pearls and opals. She had dark hair and she began to speak. She spoke in Russian: 'You have been a good cab horse to bring others to me. Now I want a ride myself. I want to come back to Liskeard.'"

Dr. Pollard was puzzled by this encounter. She knew she was not asleep, so could not be dreaming. Sceptical by nature, she spoke the following words to the lady who, as she said later, she believed to be an apparition of the Virgin Mary:

"If you are who you purport to be, I need some sort of proof that you are who you are. Visions are two a penny, and anyone to whom I mention this will think I am crazy, so before I stick my neck out for you, I ask you to stay there long enough for me to make a sketch of you. Then tomorrow I'll start painting a picture based on that sketch. I'll submit it to the Paris Salon and, if it is hung, which is most unlikely, I will accept that you are genuine and try to do something about your request."

The lady smiled and nodded her head. Dr. Pollard picked up the nearest thing to hand, an old envelope, and quickly started to draw. On completion of this self-appointed task, she looked down, and then back up to the lady -but she had gone.

The next morning, Dr. Pollard started to paint her picture. Whilst it was based on what she had seen, it was not a true portrayal of the apparition.

She painted Jesus on the lap of Mary, even though the child had not been present the previous day. In Dr. Pollard's painting, Our

Lady was seated in a dark cavern with her feet in water, rather than in her old arm chair. She also added a cowrie shell in the hands of the child Jesus. She named the water colour *La Vierge à la Porcelaine*. Many find it strange that she should paint a picture so different in form from the alleged vision. However, Dr. Pollard always went to great lengths to explain that the painting was supposed to be "a painting of Our Lady". It was not a specific representation and certainly not completed to explain her vision to anyone. "After all," she said, "It was I who suggested the painting for my own and possibly Our Lady's benefit as a proof that I had been given the mission. I always liked to see Mary painted as a "Madonna and Child", so that is how I portrayed her. My old armchair would hardly have made a very good setting so, although I drew the face and clothes as I had sketched them on the envelope, the rest was pure artist's imagination."

Having never previously submitted a painting to any exhibition, she had no idea how to proceed. However, having told Our Lady that she wanted it hung in the Paris Salon, she knew what she must do. She packed it up and sent it to the Salon. She asked if they might be interested in hanging the painting, which was not for sale, in an exhibition.

To her great surprise, she heard, in early 1956, that it would be hung in the Paris Salon summer exhibition.

She had shown the painting to no one before despatch. She did not mention either the vision or the painting until early 1956, other than to her spiritual director, Father Esmond. He advised her to notify Bishop Cyril Restiaux of Plymouth. She did, indeed, notify the bishop after first notifying Father Hackett, the parish priest at Liskeard.

When Dr. Pollard tried to speak to Father Hackett at Liskeard soon after her vision, he was away on holiday. However, an elderly gentleman, Mr Volk, who was the church organist, was present in the church. Whilst Mr Volk's connection with the shrine is not known, his eyes lit up when Dr. Pollard asked him whether Our Lady had ever been revered in Liskeard. He explained that a pre-reformation shrine was indeed present in the town and knew its exact location. He immediately offered to take her there.

Full of excitement, he immediately left his organ stool, locked the church door and they turned down West Street and walked until they reached Old Road. They then forked right before suddenly turning right again on a very sharp bend, down an extremely steep, narrow beautiful lane. Although Dr. Pollard's elderly guide fell on the slippy ground a couple of times, he did not seem the worse for wear. Eventually they arrived on a lane which, she later learned, was Lower Road. Immediately opposite her was a little gate over a stream. Behind it, surrounded by overgrown trees, was an 18th century farmhouse.

Mr Volk explained that the lane down which they had stumbled was still known as "The Mass Path". Countless pilgrims would have taken this route in years gone by, and the site ahead was their destination. The owner's grandson was present at the time and was very happy to give Mr Volk and Dr. Pollard a tour of Ladye Park Farm.

On entering the site, Dr. Pollard immediately noted a type of grotto over a stream. She marvelled at the similarities between the grotto and her watercolour, *La Vierge à la Porcelaine*. When she had painted it, she had no knowledge of this spot and certainly no notion of water there.

Two explanations of this grotto were later given. Martin Gilliat, a renowned Marianologist of the 1950s and 1960s, believed it to be an 18th century folly. However, various Christians who later lived in the house were convinced it was a baptistery, and several baptisms took place there in the early 2000s.

Here are Dr. Pollard's own words after seeing Ladye Park Farm for the first time:

"The Shrine site consists of an orchard (mentioned in ancient records) a small plain vaulted building under a grassy mound, overgrown with laurel bushes – perhaps a baptistery, at the edge of a pool. There is also a pretty well, but this is not part of the shrine. The lower storey of the chapel is built into the farmhouse. There is a bricked up arched doorway and two trefoil-headed loopholes. This was most exciting and Mr Volk was as excited as I was."

45 years later, the arch was unbricked.

Dr. Pollard was extremely impressed. This, as well as having her painting accepted by the Paris Salon, convinced her fully of her mission to restore the shrine to its former glory. However, despite her best efforts, she was unable to achieve anything over the next 10 years.

Neither finances nor church approval were the cause of this delay. It was the discovery of a covenant forbidding religious services at the spot for 400 years, which meant that nothing could happen for 10 years, until 1965. Whilst this exasperated Dr. Pollard, she was also encouraged, because she believed this to be the reason why Our Lady had waited so long make her wishes known.

1965 came and went. They still seemed to be no further forward in re-establishing a permanent shrine at Ladye Park. Dr. Pollard, accepting that God's time is not our time, wondered if her role had been to light the spark for future generations.

La Vierge à la Porcelaine by Margaret (Peggy) Pollard 1955.

Grotto over stream at Ladye Park, thought by some to have been a baptistery. Used in the late 20th century for adult baptisms.

Water flowing through baptistery at Ladye Park down
to stream below.

Full length view of Ladye Park House. Old chapel is incorporated into the left side.

The original shrine site still known as Ladye Park remains in private hands.

Pool at Ladye Park. Martin Gilliat thought it was more likely to have been the baptism pool, not what is now called the baptistery.

In 1999, a new spring appeared two weeks before a pilgrimage. A year later this leat was built to feed the spring into the pool.

Remains of 2nd millennium chapel built into
18th century house of Ladye Park.

Chapter Two
Truro

As the grand-niece of former prime minister William Gladstone, Dr. Margaret Pollard was not without funds. During the 10 years of waiting, she had gathered together enough money of her own to purchase Ladye Park. When it seemed as though her input would not be needed, she transferred her interest to building a new Catholic Church in her home town of Truro.

She had initially converted to Anglicanism and loved worshipping in the beautiful Truro Cathedral. On converting to "the one true church", as she put it, she had no alternative but to move to a small Catholic chapel on the edge of town. Ever since, she had dreamed of seeing her Lord in a more prestigious building. There was clearly a need for more space, particularly in the summer months when tourists flocked into Cornwall.

In researching Ladye Park and early Christianity in Cornwall, she came across a Medieval Guild of Our Lady of the Portal in Truro. With the approval of parish priest Father Wharton, she set about reforming the guild, with the express purpose of building a new Catholic church in Truro. The project went without a hitch. A very suitable site soon became available in the same street of the original mediaeval fraternity church. Although Dr. Pollard liked to think it might have been on the very spot, no records were found to prove this either way.

The church was to be built on an overgrown piece of ground, previously the garden of an old house. Many beautiful plants and flowers struggled for life amongst the brambles. Passing the site each morning on her way to Mass at the old chapel, a clump of irises particularly attracted Dr. Pollard. When the time came for the bulldozers to move in, she vowed to dig up the blooms and take them to her own small garden. Unable to bear the thought of them

13

being destroyed by heavy machinery, she set about extricating them before work was due to begin. She had barely begun when she struck something hard. Thinking it to be a stone, she began to dig around it. Using her other hand to ease it out, she was flabbergasted to discover a larger than life sized pottery head of a lamb. It looked as though it had broken off from its body. However, with no sign of any other pieces, she continued digging up the irises, taking them and the strange head back home.

The next morning, as usual, she walked past the new site, as she said the rosary on her way to Mass. Walking past the spot where she had pulled up the irises, she noticed that the ground seemed very wet. On closer inspection, she noticed what appeared to be a pool of water at the spot.

"Good gracious," she thought. "I must have burst a pipe when digging up those flowers. I'd better let the surveyor know."

Returning home after Mass, she immediately phoned the architect instead, who she knew personally.

"You'll never guess what I've gone and done", she said. "I think I've cracked a pipe while pinching some irises from the church site. It happened last night but there is a pool of water there now."

"Impossible," came the reply. "A complete survey has been made. There are no pipes on the land. It must be water from the river or somewhere else."

"That's the first time I've heard of water flowing up hill," she retorted. "And we've had no rain for a long time. I think it must be a spring."

"Impossible!" came his reply. "We even employed a water diviner."

"You'll have to come and have a look for yourself", she answered. "The workmen are due to start any minute."

The architect reluctantly agreed to meet her on site half an hour later.

She rushed back to St. Austell Street, where a group of labourers was already assembled. As Dr. Pollard and the architect stood over the spot in question, the pool seemed even larger than two hours before. Suddenly, with a gurgle and a "whoosh", a spring of water bubbled and appeared. They were dumbfounded. The incident was witnessed by all the workmen who were awaiting the day's instructions.

At last the architect found his voice.

"This is bang in the middle of where the church is planned", he said. "We'll have to try and divert it, but at this moment I can't quite think how."

"No fear", came Dr. Pollard's instant response. "If it has sprung up just here, that's where Our Lady wants it. We must make it into a well, a new holy well for Cornwall, and incorporate it into the church."

And that is exactly what happened. The water from it was used by Bishop Restieaux of Plymouth in blessing the church at its dedication on Thursday 17 May 1973. A lid of Cornish slate was used, on which was inscribed FONS MARIAE MATRIS PASTORIS ET AGNI: the well of Mary, mother of the Shepherd and the Lamb. This was partly a quotation from the *Akathistos* of the most Holy Mother of God, a hymn in honour of Our Lady of the Portal. This was translated from the Slavonic church by Dr. Pollard and partly remembers the strange lamb's head that was found above the spring.

The well, with its engraved slate lid, can still be found to the left of the altar in the church of Our Lady of the Portal in Truro. Most people are unaware of its existence. Although the story of how it came to appear is gradually being forgotten, Dr. Pollard was convinced that one day, in God's good time, it will prove to be a very special well. As she said, in her best "mockney" accent, which she used when communicating with the National Trust in Ferguson's Gang: "You ain't seen nothin' yet."

The rest of Dr. Pollard's life was devoted to Our Lady of the Portal and the Catholic Church. She was an expert organist, linguist, and needlewoman. She translated the *Akathistos* of the Most Holy Mother of God from the Church Slavonik and embroidered countless beautiful tapestries, one of which hangs in Truro Catholic

Church. This tapestry shows the coronation of Our Lady with a group of saints known as the "Fourteen Holy Helpers". A group of parishioners and others made a pilgrimage to this shrine at Vierzehnheiligen in Bavaria, "a jewel of late German Baroque", in 1985. The Ladye Park Pilgrimage banner is kept in Truro Cathedral. Dr. Pollard always believed that, at some point in the future, there would be a link between Truro, Vierzehnheiligen and Liskeard, but did not know how or when.

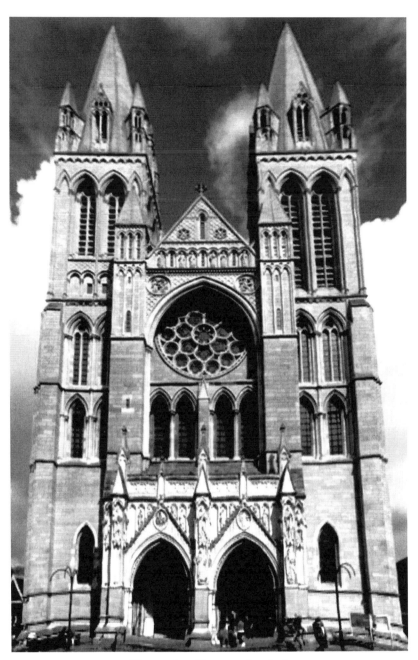

Truro Anglican cathedral

Catholic church of Our Lady and Saint Piran, Truro, dedicated 17 May 1973 and blessed by Bishop Restiaux with water from the spring. This can now be seen as a well in the nave of the church.

Sketch of original Catholic church of St Piran and presbytery from The Architect, July 24 1885. This was the tiny chapel which predated the building of the new Catholic church in Truro.

Photo of spring made into a well, easily seen but now usually ignored, in the centre of the church of Our Lady of the Portal and St Piran, Truro.

Photo showing well with slate lid carved with Latin inscription, inside the church of our Lady of the Portal and St Piran.

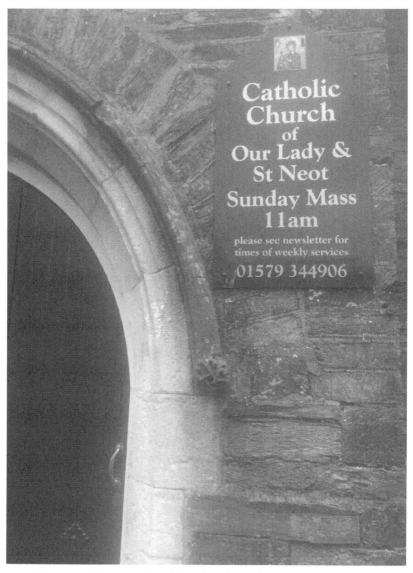

Sign outside church of Our Lady and St Neot, Liskeard.
Margaret Pollard believed one day there would be a link between
Viezehnheilligen in Bavaria, Liskeard and Truro.

Basilica of Vierzehnheiligen, Bavaria.

Life-size pottery head of a lamb, dug up by Margaret Pollard
and kept in a messy student type room until 1996.

A new spring appeared at the spot where it was found and this
was incorporated into the new Truro church.

Chapter Three
The Spark Begins to Smoulder

Whilst Dr. Pollard accepted that she was only sent to reignite the spark of Liskeard, as she said herself, "It never went away."

Whilst interest came from far and wide, it always fizzled out. In 1979, the first ecumenical pilgrimage since the Reformation took place in Liskeard. The spot was re-hallowed and dedicated as a shrine of unity. In those early post-Vatican II days, it was assumed that unity meant Christian unity. In the third millennium, our eyes and hearts are now set on world unity.

Despite the re-hallowing of the shrine, and the growth in number of devotees across the country and even the world, the original shrine site, still known as Ladye Park, remained in private hands.

No one quite knew what they wanted or expected to happen to mark the restoration of the shrine. However, there was a common belief that Ladye Park should once again become a spiritual centre and many prayers were offered to this end.

By the time Dr. Pollard died, aged 93, in 1996, the trail had gone cold. Having accepted years before that God's time is not our time, she devoted her life to her many charitable interests and the Guild of Our Lady of The Portal. Since she revelled in anonymity, much of what she did remains unknown. Years earlier, in her post-Cambridge days, she had founded the Ferguson gang, a group of masked maidens who raised money for the National Trust. All the gang had used pseudonyms. Her pseudonym was "Bill Stickers". However, until her death, when a short announcement was placed in *The Times* by an unknown person, she remained anonymous.

When restoring the Guild of Our Lady of the Portal, she stipulated that no member should be able to be identified. Instead, most were identified by numbers. There was no restriction on gender. The women were referred to as "sisters" and the men as "brothers". Only a few, mostly abroad, had the honour of being recognised by more recognisable pseudonyms. For example, there were the Roses of Africa, a group of South African nuns, Mah Enkosini, Brother Water Carrier and The Flower Mother. However, no one really knew who they were.

By the time Dr. Pollard reached the end of a very full and interesting life, she was blind and bedridden, but still mentally very alert. Parishioners and friends loved to bring her news from the parish she could no longer attend. In return, she acted as confidante, counsellor, conversationalist and more.

Shortly before Dr. Pollard's death, her friend Eirene - "Sister 13" in the Guild of Our Lady of the Portal-visited her. A child back in 1955 when Dr. Pollard was first called to Liskeard, Eirene, along with other youngsters, was taken to visit many Marian shrines, including Aylesford which, at the time, was being reconstructed. For Eirene, at such a young age, 13, the idea of a shrine in Cornwall, similar perhaps to Lourdes or Fatima, was most exciting, but those days were long gone.

Dr. Pollard told her in 1996: "You know, Our Lady still wants to return to Liskeard. I have always been like Moses, starting things for others to finish. You and your family are the chosen people. I hand the baton over to you now". Eirene was not happy. What did she mean? What was she meant to do? Dr. Pollard, sensing her disquiet, said: "Don't worry. You won't have to do anything. Our Lady will organise everything when the time comes and introduce you to the right people". Soon, on 13 November 1996, Dr. Pollard was called to her final reward. She slipped away peacefully at the nursing home where, until three days earlier, she had every morning said the rosary over the phone with "Brother 15" of the Guild. She had done this for the past 40 years.

Eirene soon began to feel a trifle uncomfortable about Dr. Pollard's words. However, she found herself, as predicted, being introduced to people with connections to Ladye Park. Interest in the pre-reformation shrine in Liskeard began to snowball.

Whilst the house and grounds of Ladye Park remained in the same private hands for a while, on the feast of the Holy Rosary October 2000 it was purchased by a Christian couple called John and Judith Wilks. They were extremely welcoming to pilgrimages and the many interested parties who turned up. Local Catholics made great effort to emphasise that the shrine was on private land and to respect the owners' privacy. The millennium year seemed to be setting the scene for great things in Liskeard. Various Christian churches erected Celtic crosses on every road entering Liskeard and the civic town council even erected one in the town centre. Artist David Whittley was commissioned to paint a mural portraying the history of Liskeard. Remarkably, without knowing anything about the recent rediscovery of Ladye Park, he recognised that devotion to Our Lady had once been very much part of Liskeard's heritage and made her shrine a striking feature of the mural.

In 2007, John and Judith felt God was telling them to sell up and move on from Ladye Park. They believed they had been sent there for a reason and their job was now done. They had renovated extensively. Initially they believed, with all the interest in the history of the house and grounds, it would quickly sell. Therefore, instead of putting it in the hands of an agent, they "spread the word". Whilst several people, both secular and religious, expressed interest, the money did not materialise, so it was eventually put into the hands of an estate agent. The agents, too, thought there would be no problem in selling. Houses in Cornwall at this time were selling quickly but, as the owners said: "Many people visited, loved it, made nice noises, but did not complete." No one could understand why such a beautiful house in an idyllic position could remain empty for almost 10 years.

Devotees of Our Lady were still hoping, believing and praying that she could be honoured at the same spot which, until the Reformation, had been an important place of pilgrimage. Many hoped that perhaps a small community would purchase and use the place in some way.

Although she tried to distance herself from all the sudden interest since Dr. Pollard's death, Eirene found herself being drawn into arranging private pilgrimages, with the kind permission of the owners, and other related activities. However, by 2013, she was tired of the whole project. If Our Lady really had asked to return to Liskeard, why was it taking so long? She could not understand. Therefore, like Dr. Pollard 50 years earlier, Eirene proclaimed: "God's time is not our time. If Jesus and Mary want Ladye Park, they have the means to obtain it without my help. From now on, I am out. Please do not contact me further regarding Ladye Park."

Celtic cross erected in the centre of Liskeard by civic council at the millennium.

Preparing for pilgrimage Mass, Ladye Park, 2005.

Prayers at Mass in Ladye Park grounds, 2005.

Blessed Sacrament chapel set up in Ladye Park House, 2005, in what was the second millennium chapel.

Pilgrims gathering to praise God at the old shrine site, 2004.

Chapter Four
A Letter Arrives

2013 was a watershed for Eirene in many ways. Despite her good health, as she was over 70, she believed the time had come to downsize her possessions in order to make her transfer to the next life as easy as possible for those left behind.

One of these possessions was Dr. Pollard 's original painting, *La Vierge à la Porcelaine,* which she had painted as her own proof that she really had been given the mission. It had come into Eirene's hands almost miraculously some years previously. However, she now felt she should pass it on to a younger devotee of Our Lady, someone preferably with children, so that it was not lost in the mists of time after her death.

Eirene was relieved when a Catholic lady who was 30 years younger than herself, and who showed great interest in Ladye Park, offered to accept it as guardian. The book, *The Lost Shrine of Liskeard*, was also out there for anyone in the future who wanted information. The picture was safe and Ladye Park was in the hands of an agent. It seemed that she had fulfilled any tasks Dr. Pollard had laid upon her. However, she soon discovered there was still work for her to do.

Around the same time as Eirene was downsizing, iconographer Patrick Tossell was visiting Oxford. In a second-hand bookshop, he was drawn to the book, *The Lost Shrine of Liskeard*. With no prior knowledge of the book, he decided to purchase it and read it on the way home.

Although he had never visited Liskeard and never heard of Our Lady of the Park, he felt, as he read the book, that he was being commissioned by Jesus and Mary to paint an icon of Our Lady of the Park.

On Holy Thursday 2015, Eirene received a letter from Patrick

Tossell, who she had never met and did not know, enclosing a photo of the beautiful icon and offering it to her as a gift for the advancement of devotion to Our Lady of the Park. Eirene was shocked and amazed. Whilst the icon was very beautiful, she had decided to have no further association with attempts to restore the sanctuary. What should she do about this wonderful offering? Eirene's first thoughts were that she could not accept the icon at that time. She would not know what to do with it. She, therefore, wrote back to Patrick. She thanked him for thinking of her, but suggested that, if he felt as though the icon was commissioned, he should perhaps keep it himself until guided as to what should happen to it next.

Two months later, having received no reply, a thought suddenly struck Eirene at Mass on 1 May, the first day of the Marian month and the feast of St Joseph.

"Our Lady has already made known her wishes. She told Patrick to offer it to you for the advancement of the cause of Our Lady of the Park. You, therefore, should accept it as guardian and wait until you are given further instructions."

At that moment, she knew she must ask the iconographer if he was still willing to give her the icon to look after until the next stage of its journey.

As soon as she had made this decision, another thought entered Eirene's mind:

"Ladye Park has not been sold and revived as a Marian centre. Perhaps the reason for this is that Jesus and Mary do not want this to happen at this time? Have we been praying against their will? There is a beautiful Catholic church in the centre of Liskeard, where Jesus is in the Blessed Sacrament. That is where Mary would want to be. Are we, in fact, meant to form a new place of devotion to Mary in the Catholic church with the icon as a focal point? In other words, should we bring people to Jesus through Mary?"

Eirene became increasingly convinced this was the case and believed that, if Liskeard church accepted the icon, everything would fall into place. She also believed that Ladye Park would be sold soon after.

With excitement and expectation, she wrote to Patrick Tossell to enquire whether she was too late to take up his generous offer. If not, she would be willing to travel to his hometown of Somerset to collect it the following weekend.

This was Patrick's reply:

"I would be delighted to hand over the icon Our Lady of the Park. It is what I painted her for and now the journey begins. It all sounds very exciting and I promise to pray for all the intentions. That is important."

Two weeks later, Eirene met Patrick for the first time and collected the icon from Clevedon after a beautiful private blessing by the parish priest, a Franciscan friar, following the Sunday vigil Mass.

The friar echoed Patrick's words, that the icon was embarking on a journey which, he prayed, would end at Liskeard. Eirene had no idea how this would come to pass. As far as she knew, the incumbent parish priest of Liskeard was completely unaware of how devotion to Our Lady of the Park had played such a great part in the heritage of Liskeard. She did not even know if he was aware there was an amazing mural featuring her in Pig Meadow Lane in the centre of Liskeard behind his very church. Nor did she know whether he was aware that Our Lady's *Fleur de Lys* featured in the town shield. She did not, therefore, feel confident to approach him out of the blue. Instead, she would hang it in her living room at home until Our Lady gave further instructions. She did not have long to wait.

On the very day Eirene brought the icon home, she received a letter from a Columban priest friend, Father Bernard McDermott.

That year, he explained, was the 1,400th anniversary of the death of Saint Columba. In researching his life, the Colombans believed it was inconceivable that he would have travelled straight from Ireland to France. He would, surely, have spent some time in Cornwall preaching the gospel. As part of their anniversary celebrations, the society, therefore, organised a pilgrimage to Cornwall to retrace the steps St Columba might have taken. It was, essentially, a private pilgrimage for Columban priests and religious and their close family and friends. Having known Father Bernard McDermott for most of her adult life, and attended his ordination 40 years previously, Eirene felt privileged to be present.

There was no question in Eirene's mind as to whether or not she would accept the invitation. Whilst she loved Cornwall, her interest now took on a new dimension. According to legend, the original shrine of Our Lady of the Park was a pagan site Christianised by the early missionaries. Since St Columba was in Cornwall 1400 years ago, it would appear conceivable that he would have been one of those missionaries. At the very least, he would surely have visited the early Christian holy spot.

Although Ladye Park and Liskeard were not on the itinerary for the 2015 Colomban pilgrimage, Eirene was convinced a short slot would be available for her to show the icon and introduce the group to Our Lady of the Park. She did not mention this to the organisers and left it to Our Lady to organise this, if it was meant to be. She packed the icon, just in case.

It then occurred to Eirene that, if she travelled to Cornwall before the pilgrimage, she could perhaps show the icon to the parish priest at Liskeard. She did not expect the parish to do anything about the icon, but felt it important that its existence be known in Liskeard. However, she discovered that the date she intended to travel to Cornwall coincided with diocesan moves of parish priests. A new priest, Father Gilmour McDermott from Truro, was taking up his position as parish priest of Liskeard and Schlerder. This, in itself, was of great interest. Liskeard had, for some years, been part of a group of four worshipping communities: Liskeard, Schlerder, Torpoint and Saltash, named "The Parish of Our Lady of the Angels, Saltash."

Bishop Mark O'Toole's decision to split the parish into two parishes, at a time when there was such a shortage of priests, seemed auspicious. Moreover, the fact that the new parish priest of Liskeard was coming from Truro, which had such great links with Liskeard, seemed more than a coincidence.

Ever since the appointment of Bishop Mark O'Toole the previous year, Eirene believed she should, at least, inform him of the interest there had been in "Ladye Park", the site of a pre-reformation shrine of Our Lady in his diocese, and to bring him up to date with recent developments.

As the date she had intended calling at Liskeard was to be the new priest's first weekend, she felt that, instead, she should write to Bishop O'Toole. She, therefore, wrote a short resume, stating how Dr. Pollard had rediscovered the ancient shrine in 1955 and believed it was her mission to restore it. She mentioned the painting, *La Vierge à la Porcelaine*, and Patrick Tossell's icon, *Our Lady of the Park*. Eirene did not mention Dr. Pollard's alleged "vision". She was aware of the teaching in the *Catechism of the Catholic Church* regarding private revelations: "Throughout the ages there have been so-called 'private' revelations, some of which have been recognised by the authority of the Church. They do not, however, belong to the deposit of faith".

Dr. Pollard's experience was definitely private. She would have balked at the idea of it being made public and would have completely rejected any notion of it being recognised by the authority of the Church. It was not in that league.

Dr. Pollard always said her call was for her alone. Each person receives a call in a different way. Some calls come through strong convictions, some through prayer, some through dreams and some are simply "known". It is said that, when St. Joan of Arc was being interrogated about her voices, she was accused in the following way: "You didn't hear God speaking to you, did you? You imagined it". "Of course!" she replied. "How else does God speak except through our imagination?"

The essential thing is to recognise our call and act upon it.

Eirene, therefore, decided that the only relevant thing to mention was that the late Dr. Margaret Pollard had been convinced she had been given a mission.

The bishop's reply was most encouraging. He suggested Father Gilmour's appointment to Liskeard could be fortuitous and that the icon looked very "noble". He suggested that Father Gilmour should be shown the icon and given the same background information as he had been sent, as soon as the priest had settled in.

Eirene was greatly encouraged. Her one aim was that the Catholic parish of Liskeard should know they had a jewel for evangelisation on their doorstep: a shrine of Our Lady, possibly the oldest in England. In the back of her mind, she knew she would love the icon of Our Lady of the Park to hang in Liskeard Catholic church to encourage parishioners, and others, to further explore their Catholic heritage. She was also aware that the church was very small and that a Lady altar was already present, with a striking statue. An additional icon, no matter how interesting, could detract from this. She therefore decided to write to Father Gilmour giving him the background, as suggested by Bishop Mark. She also told him she intended to visit Liskeard for a few days in the near future and would bring Patrick Tossell's original icon for him to view, if it would interest him.

Father Gilmour quickly replied that he was already aware of much of the story, as he had read *The Lost Shrine of Liskeard* when parish priest of Truro.

He added that, by coincidence, he had been in contact with Patrick Tossell, the iconographer at Truro. Since the Truro Church was named "The Church of Our Lady of the Portal and St Piran", Patrick had written to find out about St. Piran. He would be delighted to see the icon.

Eirene planned to drive to Liskeard for Friday evening Mass, keep the icon with her during the mass, and show it to Father Gilmour afterwards.

Arriving at the church, she noticed the baptismal font at the front of the church to the right of the altar, the opposite side to the small Lady altar. She strongly believed the icon should stand there for the duration of Holy Mass, so she entered the sacristy to ask permission. The sacristan agreed immediately. Eirene felt very heartened. She was even more pleased when Father Gilmour consented to the icon being kept on display during the Sunday parish Mass. It was also arranged for Eirene to give a short talk on Our Lady of Liskeard after the Sunday Mass. Things really were looking up. This would be the first time the parish, as a whole, would hear about their patron. She knew she had to be factual and to the point in her talk-and leave the rest to Jesus and Mary.

Here is the material from the talk she gave:

"I wonder how many of you have ever had a good look at the mural in Pig Meadow Lane.

If you have, you may or may not have noticed that it shows the history of Liskeard from time immemorial to the present day.

If you look carefully the next time you are walking past, you may notice that, to the left-hand side, there is a depiction of a chapel with a chalice in it and outside Mary stands carrying a cross.

You might ask why Our Lady should feature so prominently on a mural in the centre of Liskeard.

The answer is this: prior to the Reformation, and from the earliest days of Christianity in Cornwall, the Mother of God was revered in Liskeard under the title "Our Lady of the Park".

Liskeard became a widely acclaimed Marian centre. In 1266, by royal charter, a three-day Assumption fair was instituted in Liskeard to take place on the vigil, the feast, and the day after the Assumption. This year, 2016, is the 750th anniversary of the royal instigation of that fayre.

Our Lady's *Fleur de Lys* is even in the town shield.

At the Reformation, in the late 1530s, the shrine was closed down, disbanded and forgotten, like so many other religious sites around the country.

The reformationists were so keen to erase Our Lady from the memory of Liskeard that a covenant was put on the land to forbid it being used for religious purposes for 400 years.

Remains of the original shrine were rediscovered in Lower Road in 1956 and it was still called Ladye Park.

In 2000, David Whittley, though not a Christian, was inspired to paint the mural in Pig Meadow Lane featuring Our Lady.

In 2013, an iconographer, who had never been to Liskeard, said he believed Jesus and Mary were commissioning him to paint an icon of Our Lady of the Park."

Unframed Icon of our Lady of the Park.

On the feast of Saint Joseph, 2016, Eirene felt inspired to accept the icon of Our Lady of the Park as its guardian.

She also experienced an enlightenment that devotion to Our Lady of Liskeard should be in the Catholic church, where her son Jesus resides.

Our Lady's Fleur de lys in Liskeard town shield.

Right hand side of the 2009 restored Pig Meadow Lane mural.

The left-hand side of the 2009 restored Pig Meadow Lane mural.

Cornish warlord Carodoc in the centre of Liskeard Mural. Some have wondered whether the researcher confused Carodoc with Saint Carrock, a Celtic saint who was far from warlike.

Far left-hand corner of restored Liskeard Mural (2009) showing the Virgin Mary to the forefront and a chapel containing a chalice in the background.

David Whittley mural, AD 2000, portraying the history of Liskeard.

Chapter Five
Dreams

Eirene was grateful to Father Gilmour for the opportunity to "cast bread upon the water". She returned to Bournemouth with the icon and hung it, once more, in her living room. She knew instinctively that it should remain in Liskeard. However, she also knew that Our Lady would need to inspire her own group of devotees to work out how, if at all, the icon could "further the cause of Our Lady of the Park", as the iconographer had desired. Therefore, it was, once more, given pride of place on the wall and only pointed out to visitors.

Eirene was very preoccupied at this time. Her sister, Elizabeth, had been taken extremely ill the previous October. What started with a strange but simple illness had developed serious complications. Elizabeth had become disorientated and cognitively impaired, suffering with visual problems, lack of balance and depression. Eirene was extremely concerned for her wellbeing.

Elizabeth had a very strong faith and a particular devotion to Our Lady of the Park. As a child in Cornwall in the 1950s, she had made many visits to Liskeard with her parents. She had no doubt that Mary was present there in a special way and wanted her ashes buried in the mass path.

Elizabeth's life, sadly, had not been happy. She suffered many failures and her confidence and self-esteem had been destroyed in many ways. She felt let down, in a pastoral sense, by the Catholic Church. When she found herself in dire straits at various times in her life, it was the Baptist Church or Church of England which had come to her aid. People from these churches befriended her and her children and helped in every way possible. She undoubtedly met Jesus through these people and could not have survived without them.

Throughout this time, she still attended the Catholic church for spiritual nourishment. She loved the Blessed Sacrament and spent hours sitting, and often writing, before the tabernacle. She had no need of counsellors. Jesus in the Eucharist was her counsellor and the rosary was her spiritual link with heaven in between visits.

Then, possibly as a result of depression, she began to feel that everyone at the Catholic church she attended was talking about her in a derogatory way. She could stand it no longer and left the Catholic church to which she had been so devoted for 65 years. She joined an Anglican church, very near where she lived.

The congregation welcomed her with open arms. There is no doubt that she met the person of Jesus there amongst parishioners, as never before. They took time to get to know her, as an individual, over informal chats and cups of tea. They helped her build up a picture of her life, and recognised her many gifts and talents, particularly with children and the elderly. Within no time, she was acting as a parish visitor, helping the elderly and visiting single mothers to give them and their children support and friendship. Feeling valued, this was the happiest Elizabeth had been for a long while.

Shortly after joining her new church, Elizabeth had an operation on her foot and could not walk the short distance to Sunday services. Immediately, transport was arranged. She did not need to miss a single church celebration.

Once she recovered, she resumed her involvement in church life. She even attended prayer groups and Bible study classes, which she would never have previously had the courage to do. However, it was at one of these groups that her old insecurities resurfaced. She believed the pastor had been spreading rumours that she was too "dense" to attend Bible classes, and her only real use lay in doing the cleaning and the "dirty work" in church.

She vowed she would never go to that church again. She left and started attending another Catholic church, where she immediately felt at home. She had not realised how much she had missed both the Blessed Sacrament and Our Lady. She began to say the rosary again and gained great solace from attending adoration. She said that it was simply the atmosphere of the real presence of Christ, which calmed her every time she visited the church.

Speaking about her experience at that church afterwards, she said: "I felt at ease. I loved being there, but it was like returning to a village of one's childhood. One has happy memories. One is content to wander the lanes in the same sunshine one felt as a child, but the old familiar faces are no longer there. Everyone is so busy with their own lives that they don't notice you."

Three weeks after her sudden absence from the Anglican church, a parishioner knocked on her door. She had been missed, the parishioner said. Was she okay? She responded that she would never return to St Paul's, and related the rumours which, she was convinced, the minister and others were spreading about her. The visitor left without responding.

Two days later, Elizabeth received a beautiful card through the door, including these words:

"I am sorry, Elizabeth. I believe I have done you the greatest injustice. I do hope you will allow me to come and apologise in person."

It was signed by the pastor.

Another two days later, there was a knock on the door. The vicar stood there with a beautiful bouquet of flowers. He said:

"Elizabeth, I've come to ask your forgiveness. I did not in any way mean to offend, but I take full guilt for any words or actions I may have inadvertently used. I should have known how sensitive you feel and I should have acted accordingly. The fault is completely mine. Will you allow me to rectify it?" He then went on to ask that, in the future, if she ever felt unkind things were being said about her, she should inform him, or any member of the church team. He assured her he would sort it out. Elizabeth realised the amazing humility he had shown, especially as she knew, in her heart of hearts, that she had probably imagined it all.

He then persuaded her to return to church the following week as a one-off to give it a try. He would arrange for someone to collect her.

She reluctantly agreed.

Sure enough, a lady she knew well arrived the following Sunday morning.

Elizabeth later recalled that walking into the church felt like walking into a wall of love. Everybody she met hugged her, told her they had missed her and were pleased to see her back. A young child, whose family she used to visit, came running up to her and said:

"When are you coming to our house again?"

She was overcome with emotion, and the following week returned to regular worship at the church. Very soon she was back to full involvement, as previously.

There were a few hiccups, when her depression rose up again, causing her to "not think straight". These, however, were always smoothed over until 2015 when she was admitted to hospital with what seemed like a simple illness. She had experienced these several times in her life, but always recovered within a couple of weeks. This time, her condition grew worse and worse until all her senses became impaired. She did not know whether this was due to loss of balance or disorientation. However, she then fell over in hospital and broke her hip. From then on, there seemed to be a succession of problems.

Elizabeth was convinced they were caused by wrong medication but, once in hospital, one is in the hands of medical personnel and it is hard to question their views. Symptoms or side effects went from bad to worse. She began to experience horrific nightmares and hallucinations. Although she knew that the hallucinations were not real, they still frightened her. Night time was terrifying. She did not want to go to sleep for fear of nightmares. She became even more depressed and simply longed to die.

During this time, she continued to beg Our Lady for prayers. In her confused mental state, she began to think of Heaven as Ladye Park. On one occasion, when Eirene visited, Elizabeth said: "Just take me out of here. Drive me to Cornwall and leave me in a field near Ladye Park." When Eirene said this would not be possible, Elizabeth told her not to visit again unless she could do that for her.

Eirene returned the next day. Elizabeth was curled up on her bed in a ball and spoke of her atrocious nightmare the day before. In it, she had been left in a dark room. As her eyes became accustomed to the light, she noticed pipes all round and shelves. Then she saw there were people on the shelves. She realised they were dead and she was in a mortuary. As a nurse many years before, she knew what a mortuary looked like. Then body parts began to float from behind the pipes all round her. Many were covered in blood. Sometimes they would hit her.

Eirene just did not know what to say. She offered to pray with her but, for the first time, Elizabeth just said: "It's no use. Just let me die"

Eirene said a private prayer and left, thinking: "This must be her Purgatory on earth." It made her redouble prayers for the holy souls, realising their suffering must be even worse.

The next day, Eirene visited as usual, expecting the worst and wondering whether there was a way she could change Elizabeth's medication. Surely the medication was causing the present problems. However, what power does an individual have against professionals who are doing their best?

On walking into the ward, she was pleased to see that, at least, Elizabeth was sitting beside her bed and not curled up in a ball. In fact, there was a look of serenity on Elizabeth's face, which certainly had not been there previously.

The reason, Eirene heard, was that Elizabeth had, the night before, had a completely different dream. In her reverie, she had been walking towards Ladye Park which, in her confused mind, was Heaven. She was surrounded by the most beautiful flowers and trees. As she drew near, she could hear lots of happy voices. Then she saw people of all ages all over the garden, which full of an indescribable light, who were waving flags, letting off balloons and putting up bunting. Suddenly they began to cheer. She asked someone who was the important person they were expecting.

"You, of course", she was told.

"It can't be. I've never been important", she responded.

Then voices from the crowd began to call out:

"You looked after my children for me when I was ill."

"You visited me every day after my husband died."

"You held my hand when I was dying."

"You comforted me when you found me lost and crying as a child."

"You were the only one willing to clean the church toilets."

"I was a beggar in Truro. You were only five years old and you gave me your only penny pocket money."

"By never being afraid to speak about how much your faith meant to you, you led me to God."

From everywhere, she heard people calling out the good things she had done in her life of which she had been unaware. A group, who she instinctively knew to be holy souls, called out: "It was your prayers and fasting which got us into heaven."

Then, in her dream, she saw Our Lady coming towards her carrying a flower arrangement which, Elizabeth instinctively knew, she herself had made for the Lady altar. Our Lady was smiling and then, Elizabeth said, she woke up. Here are her words to Eirene on that day: "I've never felt so important and loved before. I didn't know I did all those things. It was such a wonderful feeling."

Stories of the nightmares had made Eirene think of Purgatory, but this dream made her wonder whether Elizabeth had had a taste of Heaven. Their brother, John, had died a few years earlier. He, too, had what seemed to be an experience of Heaven before his death. At his funeral, the following incident was related by a friend who had known him most of his life and who had spent a lot of time with him in the last weeks of his life.

John's Near-Death Story by Gus

"On 3 September 2010, John was in hospital and felt strongly he wanted the blessing of the sick. Sheila, his wife, arranged it and Father McDermott, the hospital chaplain, came to his bedside at 9pm. The next day I phoned John. He told me that, after Father had left, he had had an inexplicable experience, such as he had never had before. He could not put it into words, but it was the most wonderful encounter of his life. He said he had not been aware beforehand that he had any worries or burdens. However, he must have, because suddenly it was as though a great weight was lifted from his shoulders and he felt as free and light as air. He felt a peace, joy and contentment as never before. He also had an awareness that God was with him, which was so astounding, he felt he could simply rise up into this all-encompassing happiness. He knew exactly where he was, in his hospital bed. His Catholic religion had always meant a lot to him, but this experience, he said, was the greatest affirmation of his faith that he had ever had.

It is for me, too, as I know that John was the most down to earth person ever. He was not into emotionalism in his faith. He loved traditional prayers, such as the rosary, particularly Padre Pio's meditations. He enjoyed plain chant and visiting the Blessed Sacrament. The Holy Mass was his highlight.

I believe he was given this wonderful experience, almost a vision of Heaven, a week before he was called to his reward. In this way, no one could say he was delirious in any way, so that, in his death, he could continue to testify to the faith which meant so much to him and which he wanted to share with everyone else. There is no doubt, in my mind, that he saw Heaven where he was destined to go, but was allowed to stay to say his goodbyes. What a wonderful promotion to glory."

The day after Elizabeth related her dream, Eirene was getting ready for her regular visit. She suddenly had an overwhelming urge to take the icon of Our Lady of the Park to the hospital for Elizabeth to see. Maybe, she thought, they could say some prayers whilst gazing upon it.

She took it off the wall, where it had hung ever since it had been brought back from Liskeard.

Although she had told herself she would not hawk the image around, for some reason she believed it was important to take it to Elizabeth that day. She packed it up very carefully in a white padded freezer bag and set off.

Elizabeth was a little more confused than the previous day. As soon as she saw the icon, her eyes lit up. She extended her arms and hugged the icon as though it were a living being. Eirene quickly took it away, saying:

"Careful! You could damage it. It's not a real person"

Elizabeth became crestfallen and said:

"I'm sorry", and dropped her arms.

Eirene took the icon and placed it back in its padded bag. She felt bad that she had taken away Elizabeth's little piece of joy, but fearful that the beautiful image would get damaged.

As it was late when Eirene arrived home, she left the icon on the white sofa overnight, instead of replacing it on the wall.

Walking into the living room the next morning, she sat down on the sofa to read her post when she heard a loud crack. What was that, she wondered.

Eirene had sat on the bag containing the icon. It had snapped completely in two through the necks of Our Lady and Jesus.

Horror filled Eirene. How could this have happened? How could Our Lady have allowed this to happen?

As she tried to fix the two pieces together, a large white jagged line appeared. She panicked, but suddenly the most wonderful peace came over her, such as she had never felt before. She knew it was meant to be and was part of some supernatural plan. She sat down again and calmly prayed: "Lord, tell me what to do now."

The hardest task, she realised, was going to be telling the

iconographer. She had been entrusted with the icon for safe keeping for the promotion of the shrine of Our Lady of the Park. She had certainly not been given the icon to sit on it and break it.

She then called her husband, whose first words were: "Thank goodness it wasn't me who sat on it." He then proceeded to work out how to stick the two halves together with wood super glue, but knew it would still always be badly disfigured.

With a heavy heart, but still with an amazing peace surrounding her, Eirene wrote to the iconographer to explain what had happened.

His reply reinforced her belief that there was a plan behind the broken icon.

His words were:

"My first reaction to the news is to say the usual. Why? How? What? Then I remembered the long path of events connected with the history of Ladye Park and it certainly is a broken one. The icon is a piece of wood. The love and faith that made it and received it (you) remains unbroken. It is a test and a trial. It can be glued together, strengthened from behind, touched up, maybe, and, as we had to do with other damaged icons, put them into a nice gold frame – it does protect it, too. Our Lady will bear the scars, as do so many of her more famous images, such as *Jasna Gora* in Poland or the *Vulnerata* at the English college in Valladolid, which had arms and face mutilated and the Holy Child cut away. Yet she is loved and venerated still. God and His Holy Mother will bless you. In mending her, maybe we will experience healing -we all do need it so. So be of good heart and don't worry; 'stuff happens', as the young ones say."

Eirene felt drawn to pray for the holy souls

Our Lady of Jasna Gora

Our Lady of Valladolid

"The Mass Path, still in existence, along which countless pilgrims would have trudged in years gone by."

Christ is our bridge to heaven - the only Way across the gulf
between earthly life and eternal glory

Image by Elizabeth Wang
copyright © Radiant Light 2000, Code T-00081-OL

Chapter Six
Evangelisation

Having broken the icon, all Eirene could do was take the two pieces to a local picture framer in her town of Boscombe.

Choosing a frame was not difficult. A frame, which was one and a half inches thick in gold with a touch of silver, seemed ideal for the job. The assistant confirmed that it could be repaired with a strong wood glue which bonds the wood together.

At first, she suggested a frame which would cover the back, as well as strengthen it. However, when she saw the words written on the back, she declared that it was important that the words below should not be covered:

"Dedicated to Dr. Margaret (Peggy) Pollard and Mr Jim Ward. For the Honour and Glory of God and Our Lady of the Park."

She asked who Jim and Peggy were. Eirene replied that Peggy was a lady who had rediscovered the shrine of Our Lady of the Park after 400 years of oblivion, and Jim was a friend of the iconographer, Patrick Tossell. It was his encouragement and prayers that had brought the icon into being. He was, at the time, terminally ill. He was a devout Anglican who had travelled with Patrick to countless Marian shrines and always prayed the rosary at the annual Glastonbury pilgrimage. Jim supported over twenty charities, volunteered at a hospice, read and sang in his local church and was a huge part of village life. He was a father, widower and grandfather. On his tombstone are these words: "Friend of Congresbury, loved by all." Congresbury is the village in North Somerset where he lived. He died in Congresbury on the feast of the Holy Angels, 29 September 2013.

The date for the collection of the framed image was scheduled for two weeks later. When this time came, and Eirene had heard nothing, she phoned the shop. She was told the glue was not yet dry.

When six weeks elapsed, and still there were "slight problems", Eirene began to be concerned. She had been warned from the start that the join would still be visible and it would be best not to try and touch it up. However, she now began to worry that, in the repair process, perhaps something even more catastrophic had occurred.

Then came the day she was waiting for. It was ready.

With great haste, she made her way to the picture framer. There it was, in all its restored glory. She could not believe her eyes. It was beautiful, and the crack was invisible, as far as she was concerned.

On closer examination, she could see a tiny mark, but most people would never notice this. Praise the Lord.

Eirene looked at the beautifully restored representation of the Virgin Mary. She recalled the years when she and others were convinced Dr. Pollard had received a message to restore the old shrine of Ladye Park. They thought it would become a present-day place of devotion. She remembered her sudden intuition, only a year or so earlier, that perhaps everyone had been barking up the wrong tree. She vividly called to mind her thought that it was the Catholic church in Liskeard where Mary's son Jesus resides, in the Blessed Sacrament, which should possibly be the new sanctuary. She remembered imagining the icon as a focal point. She reminisced on the opportunity she had to visit the church of Our Lady and St Neot to share the icon and give the congregation its background. She thought back on her decision to take the icon back to her own home until it was asked for. Then she recollected the devastating accident when it was broken in two.

Suddenly Eirene felt so ashamed. How could she have been so self-opinionated as to think she should make a decision as to where the icon should hang? She should have left it for the church when she had been there a few months earlier. It was not for her to decide when the parish was ready for Our Lady. She had already invited herself, and the broken icon was a sure sign that the Blessed Virgin was taking things into her own hands. She wanted to return to Liskeard now, and the icon could be the start of a new awakening.

That very day, Eirene wrote a letter to Father Gilmour, parish priest of Liskeard, and said the icon was available for the parish if and when they would like it. She expressed her ignorance of the number of images of Our Lady there could be in a Catholic church and observed that there was already a beautiful statue of her there. However, perhaps somewhere else could be found for the icon, such as the porch, the organ loft, or St Neot's room which, in the 1950s, she believed had been a Lady chapel.

The letter was posted and Eirene waited. She heard nothing in reply but, a year to the month after she had collected the icon from Patrick Tosell, she received an email from a man called Peter Murnaghan in Liskeard. A small group of parishioners had been studying a course on evangelisation and had decided they would like to enlist the help of Our Lady. They planned to reintroduce Our Lady to the town as a first step, but it seemed that Our Lady had already had this in mind since the beginning of the millennium.

In the year 2000, the Holy Spirit was very much at work in Liskeard.

A mural was commissioned from a secular artist, David Whittley, to brighten up Pig Meadow Lane, a rather drab area of town at the time. The artist chose this theme: "Liskeard from the beginning of time to the year 2000 AD."

In the centre was the towering figure of Caradoc, an historical Cornish war lord.

One end of the mural to the other depicted scenes of Liskeard from earliest times. It showed the industrial revolution, including the discovery of tin and copper on nearby Caradon Hill, the coming of the railway, and the social and political impact which resulted. The mural portrayed local people, including a child from a nearby school wearing his millennium sweatshirt. However, the most remarkable inclusion for Eirene was that of the Blessed Virgin Mary, set in a Cornish roundhouse which, she later learnt, was a chapel. This was recording the fact that Liskeard had, at one point, been a great Marian pilgrimage centre.

Eirene had accidentally come across the mural on a visit to Liskeard. At the time, she was so excited that she contacted the town council to find out more about the remarkable millennium mural. They knew very little about it, but gave her David Whittley's telephone number. They said they were sure he would be interested in explaining more.

He was delighted to speak to her. Whilst researching the history of South East Cornwall, he explained how he came across mention of a well-known pilgrimage spot venerating the Virgin Mary "near Liskeard". He said he had an inexplicable feeling that it was very important that he included this in the mural.

Later, in 2009, he was commissioned to repaint and renovate the mural.

This time, he felt the need for slight changes. The original Liskeard locals were replaced with residents who were more up-to-date. He even included his own granddaughter, sitting on a wall in the front with her legs dangling. However, he also felt very strongly that he should bring the Virgin Mary out from the Cornish roundhouse chapel, which he had named Ladye Park, and place her prominently contemplating Liskeard's life through the centuries. He depicted her holding a cross. What had previously been a chapel was now more like a tabernacle holding the Holy Grail on which was inscribed one word: UNITY.

Seven years later, Len Fletcher from Looe was walking through Pig Meadow Lane, which he had done many times before. That depiction suddenly seemed to stand out for him. He was very interested in art and could not recollect ever having seen another painting portraying Mary carrying a cross. This struck him so strongly that he stood and pondered the sight with amazement. He went home and wrote the following reflection, which later printed in the local paper:

Looking for the Ladye: A reflection on a work of art by David Whittley

"She stands at the right side of the mural, her body turned towards the tumbling centuries of Liskeard's flowing life - down, down through the generations are revealed the events in this bitter-sweet, roller-coaster pilgrim's progress of history... on... on. towards our modern times - so much sound and fury. And there, standing centre stage, is the monumental figure of Caradoc, who like some ancient Old Testament warrior-King, stern of countenance, both hands on sword, menacingly looking at us defiantly, with perhaps even a touch of vanity and bombast - a stark contrast to the image of Mary, who seems modestly steeped in the Celtic sacredness of the natural world... of trees, water, animals and stone and who needs no weaponry... only the Word.

The expression on so many of the faces are full and focussed, the artist capturing so well the common human experiences of us all, young and old, rich and poor, at play, at work, and at war. Yet no one in this busy, bustling painting, casts a look or a glance across to that lonely Lady who, head up yet with eyes cast down, seems separated from and almost forgotten by the people in this visually arresting, fine narrative piece of art in Pig Meadow Lane.

She, Mary, is not going to preach nor plead for their attention but is just present in quiet contemplation and sooner or later they may at last notice and find her. The beauty of her stillness, her strong hands and firm steady feet, rooted in our land, suggests to me that this is an image of a woman who cannot be written out of our cultural history, that she is fully aware of the highs and lows of human experience, symbolised in the simple bare cross she carries cradled in the crook of her right arm. She too feels and shares our common humanity, such as the joy of bringing life into the world and the heartbreak of an unexpected violent death of a loved one, in her case... her Son.

We, the people, now have little or no folk memory of her since the iconoclastic repression and cultural cleansing of bygone years... but she, Mary of Ladye Park, will always be there, silently calling us back from our busy, secular lives - calling us to dwell with her for a short time amongst the greenwood and deer. She seems to whisper all through the centuries ..."Turn your heads, turn your hearts this way, look up with freshness of spirit to me and the gift I carry, for then my eyes will be raised once more to meet yours... and we will smile and all will be well... all manner of things will be well."

Rarely have I seen an artist's representation of a religious icon, Mary, depicted in this way...and I find it both moving and challenging...this piece of public art on a civic wall in Cornwall."

Len's reflection, focusing primarily on the Lady herself, made no mention of the chalice and the word unity. However, as she reread the email she had received previously from Peter and the information therein concerning the new Liskeard evangelisation group, Eirene felt that somehow the mural and the icon could be part of a plan.

Very soon after this, Eirene received another email. Peter's son was to be married in Poole, very near Bournemouth where she lived, and would be willing to collect the icon the following weekend. So, after Mass on Sunday, the icon was passed on for the next stage of its journey. Eirene met Peter and his wife and they had their first glimpse of the repaired icon, which was now securely wrapped in bubble wrap to avoid any further accidents. They said their farewells and the icon was gone.

From then on, Eirene missed being able to go downstairs in her house early in the morning, seeing it on the wall and having it as a focus for her prayers. However, she knew it was going to where it was meant to be. She felt a fluttering of excitement as it began to dawn on her that this just might be the beginning of Our Lady's plan to come back to Liskeard.

She knew that the icon, no matter how beautiful, was simply a piece of painted wood. However, after more than 50 years of waiting, it looked as though dreams were beginning to materialise, in the church rather than at Ladye Park. Soon afterwards, news came that the icon had been hung in St Neot's room of the Catholic church, once the Lady Chapel.

The weekend of 15 August 2016, the feast of the Assumption, was special for the town of Liskeard. It was the 750th anniversary of the royal charter granting a three- day fayre on "the eve, the day, and the morrow of the Assumption." A few years earlier, the town had resurrected a fayre around this time, which they called "The Ploughman's Festival". However, to the Catholics, it was an exciting rediscovery of the importance of Mary's place in the life of the town 750 years previously. They wanted to be part of this celebration and use it to make Mary's heritage known to the wider town populace. They received permission to have a stall on the parade during the food fayre on Saturday morning. They would dispense free, locally made apple juice and be available to explain the historical reasons for the fayre at that time. This was very successfully aided by a large banner and the town crier. The Catholic church, where the icon was on display, was open for visitors. Several people, who knew nothing about Mary, joined the small band of loyal Catholics who wanted to know more.

The following day, Sunday, a three-part ecumenical service in the church of Our Lady and St Neot was organised. Representatives of all faiths and Christian traditions, plus civic dignitaries, were invited to this service. The service was in three parts, with linked themes: the Church of God; Mary, Mother of Jesus; and Liskeard the Community. It was later reported in *The Cornish Times*.

At the refreshments afterwards, when visitors were again invited to view the icon, Eirene heard what sounded like amazing news. Ladye Park, which had been for sale since 2007, had been purchased by a buyer as a private home. Bees had also returned to the spot. There had been bees at Ladye Park for generations. In the end, the residents learnt to live with them until, towards the end of the 20th century, they caught a virus and died out.

In the 1950s, a farmer called Kelly lived at Ladye Park. A bank manager visited, needing to discuss his tenancy and the exact location of Kelly's boundary. He noticed that half the large room he was invited into was completely empty of furniture, as though there was an invisible barrier across it. On one side there was a dresser, chairs and a rug. The other side was completely bare. On enquiry, Farmer Kelly said: "Our tenancy only goes to that line. As long as we keep to our side, we don't get stung, The moment we cross it, the bees appear. No one has ever been stung on our side. It's live and let live, as far as we are concerned."

This seemed an extraordinary situation. However, on questioning various locals later, the bank manager discovered that the "Ladye Park Bees" were well known. Legends about them existed to the time before Christ, when the mythical Goddess Kerrid was said to have her court there. It seems that Kerrid was connected to the cretan God Ker, sometimes spelt *Car* or *Qre*. Perhaps this was the reason why it was thought bad luck would fall on anyone who managed to banish the bees. It does not explain why the bees would only sting on one side of the house. However, Eirene could not help but wonder that, throughout the time of the bees' absence, there had been problems selling Ladye Park. Now their return coincided with the sale of the house. Years previously, when Dr. Pollard was having trouble re-establishing a Christian shrine at the spot, she jokingly said: "I think the bees will have to be Christianised before our luck will change, or perhaps they could be invaded by a Christian swarm, defeated and taken over. Maybe they could then start producing Christian honey, which will not only give all the bodily benefits of health and well- being, but spiritual health too."

Now the bees had returned, Eirene wondered whether the virus had been the invading swarm and the new bees were Dr. Pollard's Christian bees, signifying a new spiritual health and well-being for Cornwall.

The year 2000, the start of a new millennium, caused a flurry of mementoes throughout the country. In Liskeard, the churches joined together to erect granite Celtic crosses at every entrance to the town. The civic council placed one in the centre near the Pig Meadow Lane mural. Some believe that inspiration for these two events-the Celtic crosses and the mural-was part of a supernatural plan for the future of Liskeard.

There was one other circumstance which, though insignificant in itself, could turn out to be another "God-incidence" in the evangelisation of Liskeard.

While David Whittley was painting a mural at Seaton Nature reserve in 1999, he was approached by a lady. She asked him if he would be willing to submit a proposal for a mural in the Catholic church of Our Lady and St Neot in Liskeard.

David was not a religious person. Although he was pleased to be commissioned, he had, at first, absolutely no ideas for the design. He was not a Christian, but he had a strong belief in the supernatural. He had the idea that all religious beliefs were, in his words, "manifestations of the same thing in different generations to different peoples." He was told that the existing large crucifix on the wall would need to remain- but that was all. At first, David had great difficulties with the design. He knew he wanted to include the history of the church, which was built by the miners, and was one of the first to be built once the restriction on building Catholic churches was lifted in 1829. However, he had no other thoughts. On visiting the church one evening, he suddenly had a feeling which he could only describe as a mixture of awe and excitement. Full details of what can only be described as a supernatural experience can be found in *The Lost Shrine of Liskeard*. He had no knowledge of Catholic theology and very little of the Bible. However, as a result of his visit, he knew, without a doubt, that the mural had to show, in some way, the transformation that man's spirit must make from an earthly perspective to the full attainment of God's domain. From then on, design ideas just dropped into place.

In the end, the church pastoral parish council, for various reasons, decided a mural was not feasible. However, it is worth recording here the design as,15 years later, David was commissioned to produce a coloured sketch of his design as a possible evangelisation tool. He named it *Vyaj an Bywnans,* which is Cornish for *Life Journey.*

Interpretation of drawing: "Vyaj an Bywnans"/ "Life Journey" by David Whittley, 2016

The design almost gives a stained-glass window effect. The surround is two granite pillars painted in a Trompé l'œil style, meaning "deceive the eye". The drawing is divided into three horizontal sections with a middle column throughout. At the top of the column is a circle of light, symbolising God Eternal. The light is directed down through the three levels, and the overall impression is one of light and warmth, radiating from heaven above down to earth.

Central to the whole picture is the existing crucifix, which is in the column of light at the middle level.

Beginning with the base level, we see, on the right side, the miners leaving the mines with their families, moving towards the light and away from darkness. Instead of pickaxes, they carry crosses, symbols of their faith and that of their forefathers, who kept it alive in times of difficulty. The crosses are also a reminder of the stations of the cross, depicting how greatly Christ suffered on his way to crucifixion. The candles on the miners' helmets convey the light of hope which burns brightly, even in the darkest places. They are coming out to build a Holy of Holies, where God can dwell amongst them. The miner, on one knee before the tabernacle, represents every Catholic who genuflects before the Blessed Sacrament, symbolising their heart bowing before the Lord, who is substantially and really present in the Eucharist.

Historically, the idea of genuflecting on one knee comes from court etiquette, and was performed when in the presence of a medieval king or noble. It was a sign of respect, as well as a pledge of service. Christians adopted this custom over time. It became fully integrated into the liturgy of the Roman Catholic Church by the 16th century.

God has always been known to Jews and Christians as the King of Heaven. To give honour to this "King of Love", Christians thought it fitting to pay respect and honour to Him by genuflecting every time they entered "His court" here on earth. This meant bending on one knee whenever they passed in front of the tabernacle. This is the receptacle in every Catholic church that holds the Blessed Sacrament, and before which a red light usually hangs. The miner, who would, of course, have known the importance of the tabernacle, is bending his knee before the King of Kings.

On the left side at this level can be seen rocks and stones strewn, some of which are dressed, ready to be used for the church building. The miners and their families are the church, as a people. It is at this earthly level that we come to understand that we are the church as a people. It is also at this earthly level that we come to understand that we are body, mind and spirit, and that human life is a gradual learning process. It is a place where we grow to understand our unique position of being touched by the light of God and formed in His image. We experience, from a human perspective, attributes of God like love, mercy, compassion, peace, truth, glory, grace and forgiveness. This, though, is nothing to how we will encounter them once the trappings of this earthly level are left behind. We need, however, to overcome human obstacles like fear and selfishness, and to work together for the good of all humanity to reach the light.

The middle level is divided by the column of light radiating to earth. This is the light of God. It flows down through Christ, on the cross, who is the link between heaven and earth. The light of God flows not only down but back up, through Christ to the Father and Holy Spirit. Each side of the crucifix shows the transition between this world and the next. The confines of earthly bodies are left behind. In a symbolic way, it shows the human spirit, or soul, gradually becoming aware of God. This is depicted by the different states of the figures that are in a kind of flux. Some are almost fully formed, whilst others are not. This is a Purgatory, or purifying state, for those who have not been drawn straight up by the light. However, here there are also God's spirits, the angels of the Lord, particularly near the column of light and the crucifix.

The top level, when examined, is subdivided. The centre is God, and this is the light eternal, shining His love down. All around, there are figures of almost pure light. They are complete. They have attained everlasting joy, having risen to the light and are at one with God. The circle of love is complete.

Depiction of Mary on 2009 restored David Whittley mural in Pig Meadow Lane, Liskeard, Cornwall.

Depiction of The Virgin Mary on
original David Whittley mural (2000).

Framed and restored icon of Our Lady of the Park.

Banner announcing 750th anniversary of the Assumption Fayre in Liskeard and proclaimed by the town Crier.

Miner genuflecting before the real presence, his Holy of Holies.

Life Journey-Vyaj an Bwynans. Coloured pencil sketch
by David Whittley.

Left hand side of Life Journey - Vyaj an Bwynans
by David Whittley.

The miners' families who are the church, working on stones to
build a church.

Right hand side of Life Journey - *Vyaj an Bwynans.*

The families of miners leaving their mines where they had
worshipped in secret. Now they are going to build a church
where they can worship their God openly. Instead of lights on
their helmets to lead the way, they carry crosses.

Sepia study for the original mural proposal on which "Life Journey" is based. It shows a soul from middle (Purgatory) level, now with glorified body, about to rise to Heaven.

Sepia study for the original mural proposal of a mother having reached the heavenly domain, and experiencing one of the many unimaginable joys. For her, it is being reunited with her child.

Chapter Seven
The Last of the Ferguson Gang

Towards the middle of 2016, a small group of parishioners from Liskeard Catholic church undertook the "Intentional Disciples' Course on Evangelisation" as part of Pope Francis' call for a "year of mercy". As a result, they were keen to reach out to the people of their great little town. They wished to continue the momentum of bringing townsfolk to Jesus through Mary, which had begun at the Assumption fayre.

A secular Cornish historical walk organiser, Brian Oldham, had shown great interest in Ladye Park, the medieval shrine site. He offered to organise a walk there for anyone in the town who was interested.

This sounded an excellent way of showing part of Liskeard's forgotten Christian heritage. The group, now calling itself "Proclaim", decided to ask Brian if he would be willing to lead a walk on 2 October 2016.

October is traditionally regarded as Our Lady's month, the month of the Holy Rosary, so this seemed a particularly suitable date. The walk took place. More than 50 people walked from the church of Our Lady and St Neot down the Mass path to Ladye Park, with the kind permission of the new owners of the property. On arrival at the garden, in beautiful warm sunshine, Father Gilmour McDermott said prayers of thanksgiving, after which the walkers sang *Mary's Hymn*, which had been written especially for the shrine in 1979 by Dr. Pollard. Visitors had travelled from as far afield as Tavistock and Camborne to join this significant event.

With the icon of Our Lady of the Park hanging in St Neot's room, Liskeard, thoughts turned to the original painting, *La Vierge à la Porcelaine,* by Dr. Pollard. It was suggested that it would be appropriate if this, too, could hang in St Neot's room, beside the icon. It had, however, been handed over after 60 years in oblivion, for safe keeping. It was felt that it was not yet the time for it to be displayed again.

Shortly before Dr. Pollard died, she was visited by a great friend. As friends do, the two swapped life stories. Dr. Pollard reminisced on her escapades as a young woman in the 1920s and 1930s as a member of the somewhat enigmatic group, the Ferguson Gang. It was the early days of the National Trust. The gang was very much influenced by Clough William-Ellis's book, *England and the Octopus,* denouncing the urbanisation of England, and the loss of so much of its heritage.

The group dedicated itself to the cause of protecting rural England and saw the National Trust as the bastion of its aim. It was an organisation in advance of its time, understanding the value of media attention. *The Times* newspaper revelled in reporting the antics of the group. If the members ever allowed themselves to be seen, they were always wearing masks, so were never recognised. One of the group, who used the pseudonym "Red Biddy", fully masked, once deposited £100 in Victorian coins on the National Trust secretary's desk and disappeared. Other gang members used these pseudonyms: "The Artichoke", "Sister Agatha", "The Nark", "The Bloody Bishop" and "Shot Biddy". Dr. Pollard herself went by the name of "Bill Stickers". During her lifetime, less than a handful of her friends were party to the secret. Donations from the gang enabled the saving of many properties, old mills, cottages, land and even part of the Cornish coastline.

The friend who visited Dr. Pollard just before she died was one of the few people who not only knew that she was "Bill Stickers", but that she had also been the leader of the gang. She therefore felt free to recall events with him. Suddenly she said, "I think it's time for a new member of the gang to be created. How would you like it to be you? And how about taking the name of "Pegasus"?"

A little taken aback, he responded, "Ok. But what would be the point?"

She replied that, after her death, she wanted him to post a letter to *The Times* newspaper. For the first time, she said, the gang would not be giving to the National Trust, but asking for their help. Although she still wished to remain anonymous, she said: "If they did but know it, they owe me a favour." She said she still believed Our Lady wanted her shrine in Liskeard to be restored and wanted to make one last effort to make this happen. She asked the newly named Pegasus to post a letter, requesting that the National Trust purchase Ladye Park, a site of great national interest.

Pegasus did send the request after Dr. Pollard went to her reward, but nothing came of it.

When, however, Pegasus, who was still alive in 2016, heard of the suggestion for Dr. Pollard's *La Vierge à la Porcelaine* to hang next to Patrick Tossell's icon, he made a decision. In the spirit of the Ferguson Gang, and Dr. Pollard's revelling in anonymity, he decided to have the original image copied by an unknown artist and donated to the church. His own artistic skill was in silversmithing, not in painting, but he knew exactly who to commission to copy the original. He asked for it to be in oils, so that the copy could never be confused with the original, which was a water colour. He then waited in anticipation for the painting to be finished, saying a quick prayer that Dr. Pollard be allowed to guide the hand of the artist who lived in China.

The painting arrived back in the UK on 2 November 2016, 61 years to the day that Dr. Pollard had decided to paint the original. Pegasus took it straight to the picture framer, who suggested a silver and cream frame. On 17 November 2016, the feast of Our Lady of Sion in France, the framed painting was ready for collection. Pegasus could only marvel at the parallel between the shrine of Our Lady of Sion and that of Our Lady of the Park. They were both situated on what were Christianised pagan sites. They were both well established as an integral part of their towns in the ninth and tenth centuries. They both had royal connections to Henry III and were both great pilgrimage spots in the Middle Ages. Pegasus realised he was probably just looking for coincidences, or "God-incidences". However, they gave him peace and confidence that this copy was just as special as the original. In fact, as he gazed on the new painting, he liked it more. The original had an impression of darkness about it, but this was much lighter. When Eirene first saw it, she was struck by the similarity of the image to the description below of Our Lady in the book written by the reputed Medjugorje visionary, Mirjana Soldo, *My Heart Will Triumph*, which she was reading at the time:

"A beautiful blueness encompassed the woman… A white veil concealed most of her long black hair... she wore a long dress that fell to her feet... Everything I saw seemed supernatural from the unearthly blue-grey glow to her dress."

Those who have seen statues and paintings of Our Lady of Medjugorje would say that the painting is nothing like them, but Eirene could not but equate that description in the book with the painting she saw before her.

Dr. Margaret (Peggy) Pollard Phd (Cambridge): musician, Cornish
bard, linguist, Christian mystic, needlewoman, translator of
Russian Slavonic liturgical documents, writer and more.

To Peggy Bland
To whom
I would have
Dedicated
This Angry little
Book
Had she been
Known to me
When I wrote it.

Clough Williams-Ellis

Inscription written by Clough William Ellis for Margaret inside a copy of *England and the Octopus,* which he gave her when they met many years after she had founded the Ferguson gang. The book was then given to Pegasus by Peggy when he was appointed a new member of the gang in 1996.

Oil painting copy of La Vierge à la Porcelaine donated by
Pegasus to the church of Our Lady and Saint Neot, Liskeard.

Copy of Benemerenti certificate awarded to Margaret Pollard by
Pope John Paul 23 for outstanding services to the Catholic Church

Three books which helped inspire this book.

Author's Epilogue

As mentioned in the introduction, I did not have any intention of writing my first book, *The Lost Shrine of Liskeard*. It simply happened.

The writing of this book has been a similar experience. From the moment I purchased my blue note book on 15 August 2016, until the end of chapter seven, it was as though I was being directed what to write. However, as soon as I came to the end of chapter seven, there was nothing.

I had heard of "writer's block". This, certainly, was it. I began to question what I had written. What was the purpose of it? Who was going to read it? There was no doubt in my mind that I had been called to write this account. But why?

At first, I had lofty ideas that I was meant to be leading readers to a new understanding of Our Lady, perhaps to pray more or even to start praying. I think I felt that this book was going to be the start of something. I am not sure what that "something" is. I began reading and collecting articles on Our Lady. I even signed up for an online course, "The Bible and The Virgin Mary", hoping to find some wise words to write. Then it dawned on me. I was not meant to be doing anything. I could not do anything. I am no theologian. I can only write from experience. Religious writing is neither my forte nor one of my qualifications.

The book which spoke to me more than anything else I read at the time, or have ever read, was called *My Heart Will Triumph* by Mirjana Soldo. It would take too long for me to explain why. I can only highly recommend you read it for yourself. Suffice to say, I realised, after reading that book, that Jesus and Mary do not want us to be anything other than who we are. They do not ask us to do anything unless they have already given us the required talents. We need to be true to ourselves in everything. We also need to trust our intuitions, as it is through them that God speaks to us.

The truth, I realised, was that this book has been inspired by four works of art: *La Vierge à La Porcelaine* by Dr. Margaret Pollard, "*Our*

Lady of the Park", the icon by Patrick Tossell; the Liskeard Council Mural in Pig Meadow Lane; and *Vyaj an Bywnans / Life's Journey,* the coloured pencil drawing by David Whittley.

No epilogue was needed, but on 18 January 2017 I read in the media of a monumental event in this secular era. Poland's government-not Poland's Catholic hierarchy-had adopted resolutions recognising Mary as Queen of their nation. It was declared that Marian devotion had a special importance for the homeland, not only because of the religious aspect, but also due to its entwinement in the social, cultural and patriotic expression of Polish life. A jubilee year was proclaimed to mark the 300th anniversary of the canonical crowning of the image of Our Lady of Czestochowa by Pope Clement XI. Furthermore, it was stated that Our Lady is woven into the entire history of Poland.

Who knows? Maybe, one day, Our Lady of Liskeard, or Our Lady of Cornwall, *Maria Wynn a Gernow,* as she has come to be known, will be nationally recognised in the same way.

Bibliography

The Holy Bible

Bagnall, P. and Beck, S. (2015) Ferguson's Gang: The Remarkable Story of the National Trust Gangsters, London: National Trust Books

Chapman, G. (1994) Catechism of the Catholic Church, London: Continuum International Publishing

Pollard, M. and Godbeer, F. (1986) Guild of Our Lady of the Portal: Dyllansow Truran

Pollard, M. and Riche, S. (1955 – 1966) Ladye Park: Letters and Research, unpublished and in author's possession.

Riche, C. (2002) The Lost Shrine of Liskeard, London: Saint Austin Press

Soldo, M. (2016) My Heart Will Triumph, London: Catholic Shop

William-Ellis, C. (1996, reprint edition) England and the Octopus, London: CPRE

www.aleteia.org

At time of printing (2018) Ladye Park is in private hands and it must be stressed access is only possible on official pilgrimages. Interested parties are asked to respect the owner's privacy.

The icon of Our Lady of the Park and the oil painting "La Vierge a la Porcelaine" can be viewed in the church of Our Lady & St Neot, Liskeard (phone for opening times), and the David Whittley mural can be viewed in Pig Meadow Lane, Liskeard.

Printed in Poland
by Amazon Fulfillment
Poland Sp. z o.o., Wrocław